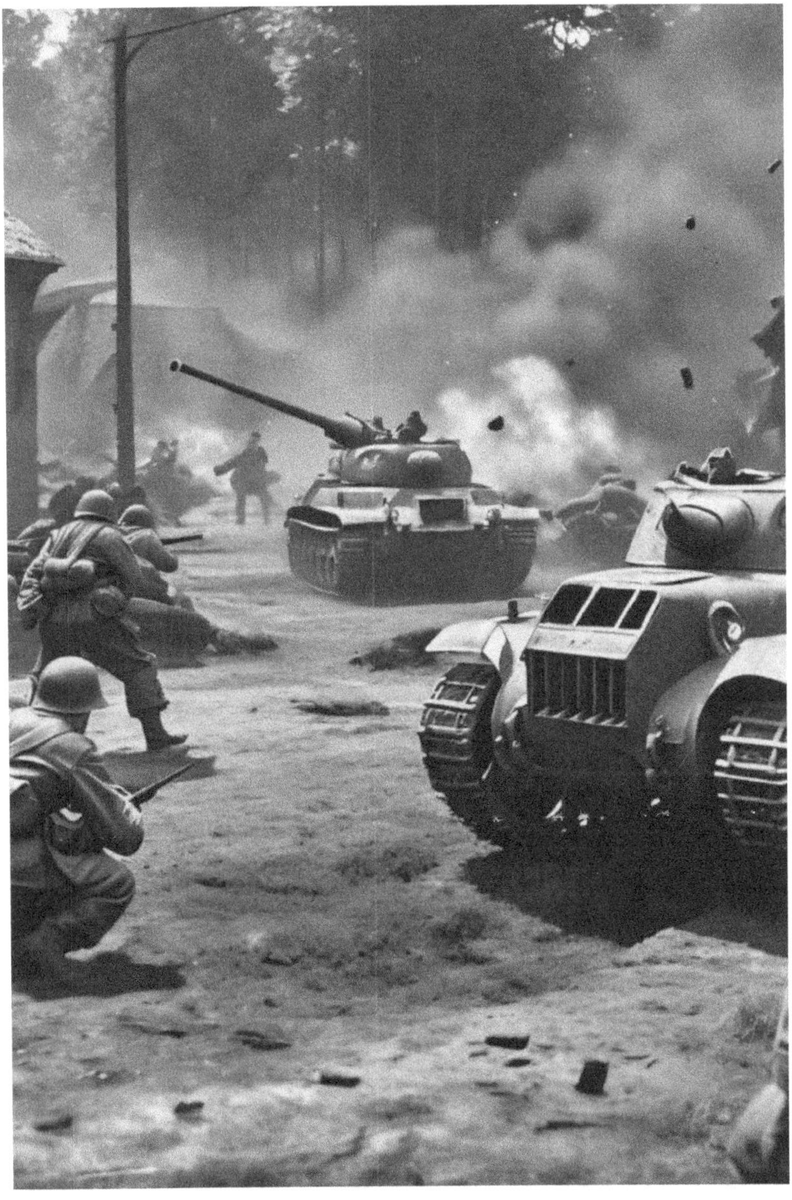

A NEW PLAYER'S GUIDE TO MEN OF WAR GAME

Beginners Tips and Tricks for Navigating Men of war

By

Ryan W. Perez

Intentionally left blank

Copyright © Ryan W. Perez, 2024

All rights reserved. No part of this publication may be reproduced, distributed, or transmitted in any form or by any means, including photocopying, recording, or other electronic or mechanical methods without the prior written permission of the copyright owner, except in the case of brief quotations embodied in critical reviews and certain other non commercial use permitted by copyright law.

Disclaimer

This book, "A NEW PLAYER'S GUIDE TO MEN OF WAR GAME" is an unofficial guide and is not endorsed by or affiliated with the creators or original copyright holders of "Men of war".

The strategies, tips, and secrets discussed in this guide are the author's interpretations and personal insights into the game and are intended to help enhance the gaming experience for players.

Table of Contents

INTRODUCTION..10
   A Glance at the Men of War Involved............................ 11
   The Road to Mastery Awaits... 14

PART 1..16
GEAR UP FOR WAR...16
      CHAPTER 1.. 17
   Welcome to the Battlefield - A Brief Overview of Men of War.. 17
   What is Men of War?.. 18
      CHAPTER 2.. 27
   Mastering the Basics - Controls, Interface, and Navigation 27
   Essential Controls: Moving, Selecting, and Commanding Units..28
   Mastering These Controls Takes Practice........................30
      CHAPTER 3.. 36
   Boot Camp: Training Your Troops - Unit Types and Roles 36
   Infantry Squads: The Backbone of Your Army................ 37
      CHAPTER 4.. 45
   Building Your Arsenal - Understanding Unit Statistics and Equipment..45

Deciphering Unit Stats: Health, Armor, Durability, and Accuracy..................46

PART 2..................54
STRATEGIES AND TACTICS FOR VICTORY..................54
    CHAPTER 5..................55
    Manoeuvring to Domination - Mastering Unit Formations and Movement..................55
    Fire and Maneuver: Utilizing Cover, Flanking, and Overwatches..................56
    CHAPTER 6..................65
    The Art of War - Offensive Strategies and Tactics..........65
    Breaking Through Enemy Lines: Breaching Fortifications, Overwhelming Defenses..................67
    CHAPTER 7..................73
    Defense: A Fortress Unbreachable - Fortifying Your Positions..................73
    Building Strong Defenses: Sandbags, Bunkers, and Anti-Tank Obstacles..................73
    CHAPTER 8..................82
    Mastering the Art of Direct Control - Taking the Wheel..82
    When to Use Direct Control: Precision Maneuvers and Tactical Advantages..................82
    The Risks and Rewards of Direct Control: PART 3........93
    BEYOND THE BASICS..................93
    CHAPTER 10..................94
    The Road to Mastery - Advanced Techniques and Strategies..................94
    Combined Arms Tactics: Coordinating Infantry, Vehicles, and Support for Maximum Effect..................94

Multiplayer Strategies: Adapting to Online Challenges
and Player Tactics.. 98
CONCLUSION.. 106
APPENDIX...110

Intentionally left blank

INTRODUCTION

As the terrain is decimated, the sound of artillery can be heard rolling over it. Tanks fight with one another in a deadly dance of steel. The infantry units surge through the smoke and fire that is around them. You are now immersed in the world of Men of War, a real-time strategy game that places you in the middle of violent conflicts that took place throughout history.

In order to successfully navigate the war-torn world of Men of War, this thorough guide will act as your vital guidance through the game. You will be equipped with the information and abilities necessary to conquer the battlefield by reading these pages, regardless of whether you are a seasoned veteran of strategy or a young recruit.

A Glance at the Men of War Involved

Men of battle is a real-time strategy game that immerses you in the turmoil of battle and forces you to make decisions in real time. In a high-stakes dance of strategy and tactics, you will assume command of a variety of forces, ranging from agile rifle squads to massive armoured tanks, and you will be responsible for orchestrating the activities of these units. You will feel as if you are there in the thick of the action thanks to the game's breathtaking graphics, which beautifully depict the brutality and intensity of mediaeval conflicts.

What This Guide Offers

This tutorial is meant to be your one-stop shop for grasping the subtleties of Men of War. We'll lead you through the essentials, from unit control and resource management to strategic decision-making and battle tactics. Whether you're confronting a hard single-player campaign or delving into the competitive realm of online multiplayer, this book will equip you with the knowledge and abilities to emerge triumphant.

What to Expect in the Coming Chapters

Getting Started: We'll begin with the fundamentals, walking you through the gaming interface, unit selection, and important controls. You'll learn how to explore the battlefield, give instructions to your soldiers, and comprehend the main principles of the game.

Mastering the Battlefield: Once you've learned the foundations, we'll go further into battlefield strategies. We'll cover unit formations, resource management, and the art of combined arms combat. You'll learn how to use the capabilities of various troops, coordinate their activities, and employ support components to achieve maximum combat success.

Campaign techniques: For single-player fans, we'll examine campaign-specific techniques. You'll learn how to alter your tactics depending on mission goals, terrain factors, and opponent troops. We'll share important suggestions for conquering hard missions and attaining beautiful campaign triumphs.

Conquering the Online Arena: Ready to test your abilities against human opponents? We'll equip you for the online combat. You'll learn crucial multiplayer methods including scouting, adjusting to diverse playstyles, and exploiting opponent vulnerabilities. We'll also address the significance of collaboration and communication to ensure online dominion.

Advanced Techniques and Strategies: As you perfect your talents, we'll expose you to advanced tactics and strategies. You'll cover unit micromanagement, complex unit commands, and the art of utilising terrain to your advantage. We'll dig into flanking operations, artillery deception, and smoke screen tactics, taking your strategic knowledge to the next level.

Beyond the Basics: This guide goes beyond the main gameplay. We'll give a unit reference guide to acquaint you with the strengths and weaknesses of various units. Additionally, we'll present a dictionary of crucial phrases used in the game, ensuring you comprehend the language of conflict. Finally, we'll steer you towards helpful online resources like strategy guides, community centres, and tutorials to continually grow your knowledge and develop your talents.

The Road to Mastery Awaits

The route to becoming a master of Men of War demands devotion, practice, and a passion for knowledge. This handbook will be your trusty friend on that trip. So, soldier, buckle yourself in, polish your strategic thinking, and ready to win the battlefield!

The booming voice of the commander booms through your headset: "Your orders, soldier? Lead your soldiers to victory!" Are you ready? Let's begin your Men of War training!

PART 1

GEAR UP FOR WAR

CHAPTER 1

Welcome to the Battlefield - A Brief Overview of Men of War

Strap up your helmet, soldier, for you're about to fall headlong into the cruel and tactical world of Men of War. This real-time strategy game (RTS) takes you right into the heart of World War II, where you'll command enormous armies in heated conflicts for territory and survival. But Men of War isn't your ordinary point-and-click RTS. It needs strategic thought, smart methods, and a good dose of micromanagement to emerge triumphant.

This initial chapter will act as your boot camp briefing, teaching you to the main principles and elements of Men of War. We'll discuss what makes this game distinctive, go into the heart-pounding action, and (if appropriate) help you pick the perfect version for your requirements. So, grab your notes and polish your pencils, because by the conclusion of this chapter, you'll be ready to organise your soldiers and win the battlefield.

What is Men of War?

Men of War isn't just another strategy game with nameless soldiers and faceless armies. It puts you into the merciless maelstrom of World War II, where every soldier under your command is an individual. You'll handle squads of soldiers, command heavy tanks and armored vehicles, and employ specialist units for reconnaissance and support.

Here's a summary of what puts Men of War apart:

Granular Unit Control: Unlike other RTS games where you command whole armies with a single click, Men of War concentrates on individual squads and vehicles. You'll directly control their movement, formations, and even take over individual troops for more accurate moves. This degree of complexity allows for elaborate tactics and plans, but also needs greater hands-on administration.

Focus on Realism: Forget base construction and resource collecting — Men of War puts you directly into the battle. You'll take critical areas on the battlefield to acquire supplies and reinforcements, but the fundamental gameplay relies upon tactical unit deployment, combined arms combat, and exploiting opponent vulnerabilities.

Brutal and Unforgiving Combat: War is no stroll in the park, and Men of War reflects that. Soldiers may be silenced by enemy fire, suffer morale decreases from significant casualties, and even perish forever. One false move might leave your whole squad exposed and defenceless, requiring you to carefully evaluate your tactics and unit placement.

Emphasis on Historical Accuracy: While not a comprehensive historical simulation, Men of War tries for accuracy. Units, vehicles, and weapons are precisely reproduced based on real-world equivalents. You'll command renowned tanks like the Sherman and Tiger, wield traditional infantry weapons like the M1 Garand and MP40, and experience the chaos and violence of historical engagements.

This unique mix of detailed unit management, historical authenticity, and a concentration on tactical fighting sets Men of War apart from the RTS crowd. It's a game that rewards careful preparation, fast reactions, and a thorough awareness of your troops' strengths and limitations.

Core Gameplay Features

Now that you have a basic knowledge of what Men of War is all about, let's go further into the major gameplay aspects that will define your experience:

Campaign Mode: (Assuming the game features a campaign mode) Dive into a narrative-driven campaign that takes you through crucial battles of World War II. You'll command various factions, experience diverse situations, and gain new troops and skills as you go.

Skirmish Mode: Test your abilities against AI opponents in customisable skirmish bouts. Choose your map, difficulty level, and factions, then wage war on a variety of battlefields.

Multiplayer Mode: (Assuming the game includes multiplayer) Go head-to-head with other players online and test your tactical ability against human opponents. Hone your talents, build innovative plans, and climb the competitive ladder.

Unit Variety: Men of War has a broad assortment of troops, from basic infantry squads holding rifles and machine guns to specialist squads armed with anti-tank weapons and flamethrowers. You'll command powerful tanks, agile armored cars, support vehicles like artillery and engineers, and even employ reconnaissance troops to spy enemy positions.

Direct Control: As indicated previously, Men of War lets you to take direct control of individual troops or vehicles. This may be vital for precision tactics like flanking enemy positions, shooting opposing tanks, or leading a daring infantry attack.

Tactical Formations: Utilize a variety of formations for your infantry teams depending on the scenario. Line formations give maximum firepower for frontal assaults, while skirmish formations provide superior protection and agility in open terrain.

Morale System: Soldiers in Men of War aren't simply robots. They might suffer from poor morale if they incur high wounds or observe friendly troops collapse. A squad with low morale is less effective in battle, so keeping your men motivated is crucial.

Physics and Destructible surroundings: The surroundings of Men of War aren't merely static backgrounds. Buildings may be damaged and destroyed, affording tactical chances. Tanks may crash through barriers, artillery fire can produce craters, and explosions can send debris flying. This amount of destructibility provides an element of realism and enables for imaginative problem-solving on the battlefield.

Weapon Effects and Ballistics: Bullets are modeled with accurate trajectory and penetration. This means aiming matters. A well-placed shot may knock down an opposing soldier instantaneously, while a poorly aimed one can merely graze their helmet. Similarly, various weapon kinds have distinct impacts. A machine gun could subdue and hold down adversaries, whereas a tank cannon can annihilate them in a single blow. This adds dimension to battle and rewards smart placement and precise shooting.

Beyond the Basics

Men of War provides a plethora of features outside the primary gameplay loop. Here are some more components that add intricacy and depth to your experience:

Leader Units: Certain units, frequently officers, grant leadership bonuses and unique powers to adjacent soldiers. Keeping your commanders alive and well-positioned may dramatically improve your army's morale and performance.

Veterancy System: As troops survive fights and gather experience, they become veterans. Veterans are more precise, resilient, and have better morale, making them essential assets on the battlefield.

Command Voice System: Give clear and simple instructions to your forces utilising the in-game voice command system. You may instruct them to move, attack, maintain position, or even employ certain equipment.

Choosing Your Edition (if applicable)

If Men of War has numerous versions available, picking the proper one might be daunting. Here's an overview of things to consider:

Base Game: The core experience includes the original story and multiplayer modes. This is a fantastic beginning place for new players.

Deluxe Edition: May contain more campaign objectives, bonus units, or cosmetic stuff like skins for troops or vehicles. Consider this if you want extra material after finishing the main game.

Gold Edition: Often the most extensive edition, featuring all the material from prior editions, including more campaigns, bonus units, maps, and maybe even access to the game's soundtrack or digital artbook. This is suitable for gamers that want the whole Men of War experience.

Remember, these are only broad principles. Always verify the precise specifics of each edition before buying to guarantee you're receiving the information you seek.

This finishes our introductory investigation of Men of War. By now, you should have a thorough knowledge of the game's main principles, gameplay elements, and (if appropriate) the numerous versions available. In the following chapter, we'll go further into the nitty-gritty, learning the fundamental controls, navigating the user interface, and becoming comfortable controlling your forces on the battlefield. So stay tuned, soldier, your trip into the realm of Men of War is just starting!

CHAPTER 2

Mastering the Basics - Controls, Interface, and Navigation

Welcome return, soldier! Now that you've understood the essential ideas of Men of War, it's time to get your hands dirty and learn the tools of the trade. This chapter will lead you through learning the fundamental controls, navigating the user interface like a pro, and controlling the camera to maintain optimal situational awareness on the battlefield.

Essential Controls: Moving, Selecting, and Commanding Units

Men of War needs exact control over your forces. Here's a rundown of the main controls you'll need to master:

Unit Selection:

Single Unit: Left-click on a unit to select it.
    numerous troops: Hold down the left-click and drag a box around numerous troops to select them all.

Squad Selection: Press the specified hotkey (typically the number keys 1-9) to choose a certain squad you've set to that key.

Movement: Right-Click go: Right-click on a spot on the map to command your chosen troops to go there.

Shift + Right-Click Attack: Hold Shift while right-clicking on an enemy unit or location to direct your troops to attack.

Hotkeys: Utilize hotkeys for common movement commands like advance, maintain position, and retreat. These may dramatically increase your response speed and tactical versatility.

Formations:

Formation Hotkeys: Use specific hotkeys (typically F1-F10) to direct your infantry units into various formations, such line formations for frontal assaults or skirmish formations for open terrain.

Direct Control:

Tab Key: Press Tab to cycle among individual units within a specified group. This enables you to take direct control of a select unit for more accurate moves.

WASD Keys: While in direct control mode, use the WASD keys to manoeuvre the unit directly. You may also use the mouse to target the unit's weapon.

Mastering These Controls Takes Practice

Don't be discouraged if these controls seem overwhelming at first. Experimenting in a low-pressure skirmish versus easy AI may dramatically enhance your comfort level. As you practice, these controls will become second nature, enabling you to respond rapidly and effectively in the heat of combat.

Understanding the User Interface: Menus, Resource Management, and Unit Information

The user interface (UI) in Men of War offers all the vital information you need to control your armies and make smart choices. Let's break down the important elements:

Top Bar: Minimap: This gives a strategic perspective of the battlefield, enabling you to see the full map, friendly and enemy unit placements, and capture spots.

Resources: Keep a check on your resources, often expressed as people and munitions. Manpower affects how many troops you may reinforce, whereas ammunition are required for vehicles, artillery, and some infantry weapons.

Command Points (if applicable): Some game types could employ command points for unique powers or calling in reinforcements.

Objectives: The current objectives of the operation will be presented here, reminding you of your aims.

Bottom Bar: (May change based on the game mode)

Selected Unit Information: This panel reveals vital information about your presently selected units, like health, ammo, morale, and veterancy level.

Squads and Vehicles: This area gives a rapid overview of all your squads and vehicles on the battlefield, enabling you to swiftly swap between them.

Command Panel: Here you'll find buttons for providing basic instructions like move, assault, maintain position, and retreat. You could also discover buttons for particular unit skills or formations.

Taking Advantage of Information

The UI is your window into the situation of the battlefield. Regularly peek at the minimap to keep informed of opponent movements and take areas. Monitor your resource levels to ensure you can replenish your soldiers and sustain firepower. By successfully using the UI, you may make educated judgements, respond fast to changing conditions, and finally win victory.

Mastering the Camera: Zooming, Rotating, and Following the Action

Men of War enables you to control the camera to maintain maximum situational awareness. Here's how:

Mouse Scrolling: Scroll your mouse wheel in and out to zoom the camera closer or away from the action. Zoom in for exact unit control and micro-management, or zoom out for a larger tactical perspective of the battlefield.
WASD Keys (Edge Scrolling): Hold down the right mouse button and use the WASD keys to move the camera around the map. This helps you to follow the action even when zoomed in.

Centering on chosen Units: Double-click on a chosen unit or squad to rapidly focus the camera on their location. This is vital for swiftly responding to threats or tracking the action during intensive combat.

Camera Hotkeys (if applicable): Some games could feature specialised hotkeys for zooming in and out, moving the camera, or concentrating on particular places on the map. Familiarize oneself with these hotkeys if accessible, since they may considerably increase your efficiency.

Mastering the Camera is an Ongoing Process

Learning to use the camera efficiently requires practice. Experiment with various zoom levels and camera angles to see what works best for you in different scenarios. Remember, a strong balance between zoomed-in tactical control and zoomed-out strategic awareness is vital to success.

Putting it All Together

By learning the key controls, comprehending the user interface, and managing the camera properly, you'll get the basis for successful command in Men of War. These talents will enable you to give accurate instructions, manage your resources properly, and retain situational awareness - all critical aspects for winning success on the battlefield.

In the following part, we'll dig into the heart and soul of Men of War — the numerous units at your disposal. We'll investigate infantry squads, powerful vehicles, and specialized support units, understanding their strengths, limitations, and responsibilities in your broad tactical schemes.

CHAPTER 3

Boot Camp: Training Your Troops - Unit Types and Roles

Soldier, you've mastered the controls, navigated the UI, and learned to keep your eye on the battlefield. Now it's time to construct your army! Men of War provides a broad selection of troops, each with its own strengths, limitations, and role to play in your tactical tapestry. In this chapter, we'll study the main unit types, from the adaptable infantry squads providing the backbone of your army to the strong vehicles and specialist support units that may shift the balances of combat in your favor.

Infantry Squads: The Backbone of Your Army

Infantry squads are the workhorses of any army in Men of War. They constitute the forefront of your troops, taking objectives, fighting in firefights, and securing vital locations. Here's a summary of the many sorts of infantry teams you'll encounter:

Riflemen Squads: The most popular and adaptable infantry unit. Armed with guns and explosives, they're effective in most scenarios. Utilize them for flanking movements, holding objectives, and suppressing opposing positions.

Machine Gun Squads: Lay down a torrent of bullets with these heavy weapon experts. Their machine guns can crush opposing soldiers on open territory, but they're susceptible to flanking assaults and lack mobility. Use them in defensive positions or to pin down oncoming opponents.

Anti-Tank Squads: Equip these men with specialist weapons like rocket launchers or Panzerfausts to oppose enemy armor. They're vital for bringing out tanks and armored vehicles, but susceptible to hostile troops in close quarters. Use them tactically with riflemen for combined weapons tactics.

Specialists Squads: Certain factions could have access to specialist infantry troops like flamethrower squads or sniper teams. These units thrive in specialised settings but are frequently restricted in quantity. Utilize them strategically to exploit enemy weaknesses.

Infantry Squad Tips:

Cover is King: Infantry exposed on open terrain are easy targets. Utilize structures, trenches, and natural cover to enhance your squads' survival.
Fire and Maneuver: Don't simply stand and fight. Suppress enemy positions with machine

guns while flanking them with riflemen. Coordinate moves to overwhelm your opponent.

Morale Matters: Low morale may hinder your infantry's effectiveness. Keep your squads well-supplied, minimise severe losses, and employ leader units to enhance morale.

Vehicle Warfare: Tanks, Armored Cars, and Support Vehicles

Vehicles are the big hitters of Men of War, capable of delivering catastrophic damage and bursting through opposing lines. However, they're also costly to install and prone to specialised dangers. Here's a breakdown of the primary vehicle types:

Tanks: The greatest icon of armored combat. Tanks feature tremendous firepower and high armor, making them perfect for frontal assaults and smashing past opposing defenses. However, they're sluggish, costly, and susceptible to flanking maneuvers and well-placed anti-tank armament.

Armored Cars: Offering a mix between speed and firepower, armored vehicles are good for reconnaissance, flanking movements, and harassing enemy positions. They're not as strongly armored as tanks and may be susceptible to concentrated fire.

assistance Vehicles: These vehicles offer critical combat assistance. Look out for armored personnel carriers (APCs) to carry soldiers, artillery vehicles for long-range bombardment, and anti-air units to counter enemy aircraft (if relevant).

Vehicle Warfare Tips:

Combined Arms: Don't send tanks in alone. Utilize troops to screen them from hostile anti-tank guns and bolster their progress.

Utilize Cover: Even tanks may be disabled by focused fire. Use structures, terrain features, and smoke grenades to shelter your vehicles during confrontations.

Prioritize Targets: Focus your tank fire on high-value targets like opposing tanks and artillery. Don't spend ammo on inferior soldiers unless absolutely necessary.

Recon and Support Units: Scouts, Artillery, and Engineers

While soldiers and vehicles constitute the basis of your army, specialist support units play a critical part in attaining victory. Here are some critical support units to consider:

Scout Units: These lightly armored vehicles or infantry units excel in scouting opponent locations and uncovering their vulnerabilities. Utilize them to acquire tactical advantages and organise your assaults appropriately.

Artillery: Rain down damage from afar with artillery forces. They may blast hostile locations, soften fortifications, and disrupt opposing formations. However, artillery is immovable and exposed to counter-battery fire.

Engineers: These vital personnel can repair broken vehicles, create rudimentary fortifications, and place explosives to demolish opposing defenses. Utilize them wisely to sustain your armored army and break opposing strongholds.

Support Unit Tips:

Scouting is Key: The more you know about your enemy's locations and troops, the better. Utilize scouts aggressively to achieve a tactical edge.

Artillery Positioning: Place your artillery units tactically behind cover, preferably out of range of opposing counter-battery fire. Use them to bolster your offensives and disrupt opposing deployments.

Engineer Priorities: Prioritize rebuilding your own damaged tanks and vehicles. Utilize engineers aggressively to remove mines and demolish opponent defences.

Building a Cohesive Force

The key to success in Men of War is on creating a balanced and cohesive army. Don't depend entirely on tanks or troops. Utilize a combination of unit types to exploit opponent vulnerabilities and counter their strategy. Here are some extra guidelines for constructing your army:

Consider the Map: Open maps encourage mobility forces like armored vehicles and long-range artillery. Urban areas necessitate strong infantry with close-quarters capability.

Learn Unit Statistics: Each unit has distinct strengths and limitations. Familiarize yourself with their health, armor, firepower, and range to deploy them efficiently.

Experiment and Adapt: Don't be scared to experiment with various unit combinations. Observe what works and change your strategy depending on the opponent force composition and battlefield layout.

The Road to Victory Starts Here

By learning the many sorts of troops, their functions, and some fundamental deployment techniques, you've made a huge step towards mastering the art of battle in Men of battle. In the following chapter, we'll go further into the nuances of unit administration, covering unit statistics, equipment breakdowns, and how to successfully counter varied opposing forces. Remember, soldier, knowledge is power - and with the appropriate information, you'll be well on your way to leading your men to triumphant victory!

CHAPTER 4

Building Your Arsenal - Understanding Unit Statistics and Equipment

Soldier, you've collected your soldiers — a diversified army ready to take the battlefield. But before you unleash them onto your opponents, you need to comprehend the tools at their disposal. In this chapter, we'll dig into the realm of unit statistics and equipment, studying the data and minutiae that determine your army's capabilities. This information will be your armoury, enabling you to pick the proper tool for the task and defeat any hostile force with strategic precision.

Deciphering Unit Stats: Health, Armor, Durability, and Accuracy

Every unit in Men of War comes with a stat sheet, an analysis of their strengths and shortcomings. Understanding these numbers is vital for deploying your forces successfully. Here are some critical facts to pay special attention to:

Health: This measures the unit's overall survival. A unit with little health is readily destroyed, whereas units with high health may resist substantial punishment.

Armor: This stat determines a unit's resistance to several forms of harm. Heavy armor defends against tank shells and explosives, whereas lesser armor could only give protection from small weapons fire.

Firepower: This indicates the unit's offensive capabilities, commonly measured in damage per second (DPS). High firepower troops may swiftly inflict massive fatalities, whereas low firepower units struggle to cause considerable damage.

Range: This represents the effective range at which a unit's weapon may accurately engage targets. Don't spend your riflemen on distant foes if they lack the range to be successful.

Accuracy: This characteristic represents the unit's ability to strike their target regularly. Veteran troops often claim superior accuracy than untrained recruits.

Stats in Action

Understanding how these data interact is crucial. A fully armored tank could have tremendous HP, but it can lack the precision to fight troops at long range. Conversely, a squad of riflemen could be incredibly accurate, but their low health renders them susceptible to concentrated fire. By evaluating these information, you may make educated judgements regarding unit deployment, target selection, and tactical moves.

Equipment Breakdown: Rifles, Machine Guns, Cannons, and Explosives

Men of War contains a varied selection of weapons, each with its unique strengths and drawbacks. Here's a general summary of the most popular equipment types:

Rifles: The standard weapon for most infantry teams. Rifles are effective at medium range, although their damage output is lesser compared to heavier weapons.

Machine Guns: Lay down a torrent of gunfire with these lethal weapons. They excel in suppressing enemy positions and inflicting large losses in close quarters, but their accuracy decreases at longer ranges.

Grenades: These explosive weapons are important for clearing buildings, flushing out enemy positions, and disabling weakly armored vehicles. However, be wary of friendly fire, since grenades might damage or kill your own soldiers.

Anti-Tank Weapons: Units armed with rocket launchers, Panzerfausts, or comparable armament are important for bringing down opposing armor. However, they are frequently susceptible in close quarters and need cautious placement.

Tank guns: The main armament of tanks, these guns may decimate hostile vehicles and fortifications. However, their rate of fire could be slower compared to machine guns, and they can need precision targeting for optimal efficacy.

Artillery: These long-range weaponry pour down havoc from afar. They can bombard enemy locations and weaken fortifications, but they are stationary and susceptible to counter-battery fire.

Mastering Your Equipment

Don't only depend on the basic numbers — experiment with your troops' equipment in controlled conditions. Learn the effective range of their weapons, the area of impact of their grenades, and the reload times of their firearms.

This practical understanding will be helpful in the heat of combat.

Choosing the Right Tool for the Job: Countering Enemy Forces Effectively

Now that you understand unit numbers and equipment, it's time to learn how to employ this information to oppose opposing troops successfully. Here's how to tackle various enemy unit types:

Troops: Utilize cover, flanking movements, and superior firepower to crush opposing troops. Suppress them with machine guns, outflank them with riflemen, and deploy grenades to clear them out of structures.

Tanks: Don't confront tanks head-on with inferior troops. Utilize anti-tank experts, flanking tactics, and well-placed mines to cripple opposing armor. Coordinate artillery attacks or airstrikes (if appropriate) to take down highly armored vehicles.

Armored Cars: Their speed makes them challenging targets. Utilize cover and concentrate fire to take them down. Anti-tank weapons and well-placed mines are also useful against armored automobiles.

Artillery (Continued): infiltrating troops to seize or destroy opposing artillery pieces.

Beyond Basic Counters

Remember, these are only broad principles. As you battle various enemy groups, you'll find distinct troop kinds with particular powers. Experiment and change your tactics depending on the individual opponent force composition. Here are some extra techniques for opposing enemy troops effectively:

Intelligence is Key: Utilize recon troops and seized enemy equipment to collect information on adversary strengths and vulnerabilities. This insight will help you design your counter-strategies.

Combined Arms: Don't depend only on one troop type to oppose another. Utilize a variety of troops to exploit opponent vulnerabilities. For example, utilise infantry to suppress enemy positions while flanking with anti-tank troops to take out their armor.

Learn from Your Mistakes: Analyze your losses and pinpoint what went wrong. Did you misjudge the enemy's firepower? Did you overlook to flank their positions? Use these experiences to enhance your strategies and become a more competent commander.

The Art of War: Mastering the Battlefield

By knowing unit numbers, equipment capabilities, and viable counter-strategies, you've made a huge step towards controlling the battlefield in Men of War. Remember, the most potent weapon in your armoury is your tactical mind. Use your expertise, adapt to changing scenarios, and exploit opponent vulnerabilities – and victory will be yours for the taking.

In the following chapter, we'll dig into the heart of conflict, covering tactical movements, formation methods, and the art of flanking and combined weapons warfare. We'll provide you with the expertise to organise stunning assaults and earn decisive triumphs!

PART 2

STRATEGIES AND TACTICS FOR VICTORY

CHAPTER 5

Manoeuvring to Domination - Mastering Unit Formations and Movement

Now it's time to unleash them on the battlefield! But merely hurling your forces at the adversary won't ensure success. In Men of War, success rests on understanding tactical mobility, employing formations efficiently, and exploiting opponent vulnerabilities via moves like flanking and overwatch. This chapter will convert you from a raw recruit into a seasoned commander, planning operations that spell disaster for your foes.

Fire and Maneuver: Utilizing Cover, Flanking, and Overwatches

In Men of War, sheer force seldom triumphs. It's a game of tactical movement, where placement and tactics are vital to victory. Here are the key elements of successful combat:

Cover is King: Exposing your soldiers on open terrain is a recipe for catastrophe. Utilize structures, trenches, natural cover, and smoke grenades to hide your men from enemy fire while boosting their survival.

Flanking Maneuvers: Don't assault your adversary head-on. Utilize flanking tactics to strike their vulnerable flanks or rear. This focuses your firepower and reduces your own fatalities.

The Art of Overwatch: Position assigned troops to cover certain regions of the battlefield. These units will automatically attack any enemy targets inside their range of vision, offering critical assistance for your advancing forces.

Putting it into Practice:

Imagine you're invading an opposing fortress. Here's how these concepts come into play:

1. Utilize cover: Move your infantry squads from building to building, reducing their exposure to enemy fire.
2. Plan your flank: Send a squad or two to loop around the opposing position, hoping to strike their rear.
3. Overwatch for support: Place a machine gun unit in a strategic area to block enemy fire while your main army approaches.
4. Coordinate the attack: Once your flanking force is in place, unleash a coordinated assault from both directions, overwhelming the opponent and seizing the objective.

Mastering these ideas requires practice. Experiment in skirmishes, explore various flanking paths, and employ overwatch effectively. As you acquire expertise, your movements will grow more intricate, resulting to decisive triumphs.

Formations for Different Situations: Line, Column, and Skirmish Formations

Men of War provides many formations for your infantry units, each with its own pros and weaknesses. Here's a breakdown of the key formations:

Line Formation: A typical formation with troops shoulder-to-shoulder. It gives maximum firepower for frontal assaults but leaves your sides open and provides minimal protection. Utilize this arrangement when overwhelming firepower is essential, such during a frontal attack against reinforced positions.
Column Formation: Units are stacked in a single file line. This arrangement is good for passing

through tiny passageways or reducing your footprint while crossing broad territory. However, it delivers little firepower and renders your forces susceptible to flanking assaults. Use this arrangement for fast deployments or while going past choke spots.

Skirmish Formation: Units spread out in a loose formation, allowing some cover and flexibility on open terrain. This configuration enables individual troops to take shelter behind obstacles and offers some protection from artillery fire. Utilize this configuration while pushing over broad areas or scouting enemy locations.

Choosing the Right Formation:

The ideal formation depends on the context. Here are some other considerations:

Terrain: Line formations are better suited for open terrain, while skirmish formations are suitable for more open or broken ground.

opposing Position: Utilize line formations to overwhelm opposing positions head-on, while skirmish formations are excellent for flanking movements.

Unit Type: Machine gun squads are most successful in line formations, while riflemen benefit from the protection and flexibility of skirmish formations.

Mastering formations demands practice. Experiment with each formation in various conditions, and learn to transition between them fast to respond to the shifting battlefield dynamics.

Mastering Movement Techniques: Advance, Hold Position, and Retreat Orders

Men of War features a number of movement commands that enable you to direct your forces with precision. Here's a summary of the important movement techniques:

Advance: The fundamental movement command, commanding your troops to march towards a defined position. Utilize this command to assault targets, take important sites, or reinforce threatened positions.

Hold Position: Order your forces to stand put and return fire on any enemy threats. This is crucial for securing seized objectives, defending critical areas, or setting up overwatch positions.

Retreat: Instruct your soldiers to fall back to a chosen place or friendly lines. Utilize this order to retreat from lost fights, regroup after high losses, or lure foes into a trap.

Beyond Basic Commands:

While these are the main movement instructions, there's more to consider:

Double-Clicking (Continued): soldiers to advance there at a quicker tempo, excellent for swiftly reinforcing endangered positions or flanking actions.

Shift-Clicking: Hold Shift while clicking on a place to direct your troops to attack any enemy they find on the route. This is important for clearing structures or scouting enemy locations in force.

Hotkeys: Utilize hotkeys for commonly used movement commands like advance and maintain position. This enables for quicker reflexes and more effective battlefield control.

Movement and Positioning are Key

Mastering movement tactics and formations is important for success in Men of War. Don't simply advance your men in a straight line — employ cover, seize flanking possibilities, and adjust your formations dependent on the scenario. Remember, a well-positioned and agile force is significantly more effective than a static one.

The Art of Combined Arms Warfare

Men of War supports combined weapons tactics, where multiple unit types cooperate together to gain victory. Here are several examples:

troops and Tanks: Utilize troops to cover your tanks from hostile anti-tank weapons as they lead the attack.

Machine Guns and Riflemen: Suppress enemy positions with machine guns while flanking them with riflemen for a deadly combined strike.

Artillery and soldiers: Soften opponent fortifications with artillery fire before putting in your soldiers to conquer the goal.

Experiment and Adapt

There's no one "best" tactic in Men of War. Experiment with varied formations, movement tactics, and combined weapons methods. As you meet different terrain, opponent factions, and combat conditions, change your strategies to exploit enemy vulnerabilities and gain victory. Don't be scared to learn from your errors and modify your strategy depending on your experiences.

The Road to Mastery

By mastering movement methods, formations, and the art of combined weapons battle, you've made a huge stride towards becoming a strong leader in Men of War. Remember, the battlefield is a dynamic setting. Adapt to shifting scenarios, outmaneuver your opponent, and apply your tactical skills to gain triumphant victory!

In the following chapter, we'll dig into the subtleties of advanced tactics, analysing techniques for particular scenarios including urban warfare, armored assaults, and defensive maneuvers. We'll equip you with the knowledge to win any battlefield and outwit any opponent!

CHAPTER 6

The Art of War - Offensive Strategies and Tactics

This chapter will provide you with the knowledge to launch deadly offensives, penetrate opposing defenses, and declare victory on the battlefield. We'll study offensive plans and tactics, from painstaking preparation to the terrible reality of urban combat.

Planning Your Assault: Scouting, Objective Prioritization, and Force Concentration

A successful assault rests on thorough preparation. Before you release your soldiers, consider these vital steps:

Scouting is Key: Utilize recon troops to collect information on enemy locations, fortifications, and force deployments. Identify weak places in their defenses and organise your assault appropriately.

Prioritize goals: Not all goals carry equal worth. Focus on seizing important sites that dominate the battlefield, cut off enemy reinforcements, or give flanking chances.

Force Concentration: Don't scatter your troops thin. Concentrate your firepower on a single location to overwhelm opposing defenses and make breakthroughs.

Planning in Action:
Imagine you're charged with seizing a highly entrenched enemy town. Here's how planning comes into play:

1. Scout the town: Send in recon forces to determine enemy locations, strongpoints, and possible flanking routes.
2. Prioritize objectives: Focus on seizing the town center and vital bridges to cut off enemy reinforcements and isolate their troops.
3. Concentrate your forces: Launch a concerted attack on the weakest spot in the opposing fortifications, employing combined weapons tactics to overrun their positions.

Remember, a well-planned attack is half the fight won.

Breaking Through Enemy Lines: Breaching Fortifications, Overwhelming Defenses

Even the most well-planned onslaught will find opposition. Here's how to defeat opponent defenses and accomplish a breakthrough:

Breaching Fortifications: Enemy strongholds could be fortified by barbed wire, minefields, and bunkers. Utilize engineers to remove mines, artillery to weaken fortifications, and specialty forces like flamethrower squads to wipe out entrenched positions.

Overwhelming Defenses: Don't squander life on frontal assaults against strongly defended fortifications. Utilize flanking manoeuvres, artillery barrages, and combined weapons tactics to overwhelm enemy defenses and create an opening for your main force.

Smoke for Cover: Utilize smoke grenades to hide enemy positions and shelter your advancing soldiers during attacks.

Breaking Through in Practice:

Imagine your attack on the walled town is stopped. Here's how to break through:

1. Target fortifications: Focus your artillery fire on critical enemy locations like bunkers and machine gun nests.

2. Flank the opponent: Send a squad or two to loop around the opposing fortifications, hoping to assault their rear and create a distraction.

3. Breach and clear: Utilize engineers to remove mines and barbed wire, then send in troops with grenades and flamethrowers to take out remaining enemy resistance.

Remember, a successful breakthrough takes a mix of strategies and reacting to the environment.

Urban Warfare: Clearing Buildings, Securing Objectives in Tight Spaces

Urban areas provide particular issues. Here's how to fight successfully at close quarters:

Clearing Buildings: Utilize grenades to flush out enemy positions. Follow up with close-quarters battle with riflemen and machine gun teams. Be wary of friendly fire, since grenades may harm or kill your own soldiers inside structures.

Securing Objectives: Once a building is eliminated, continue on to secure the next target point by point. Utilize flanking moves inside buildings to avoid being trapped down.

Infantry is King: Tanks and vehicles are less effective in urban situations owing to restricted space and the availability of cover. Focus on employing well-equipped infantry teams for optimum efficiency.

Urban Warfare in Action:

Imagine your soldiers are entrusted with seizing a sequence of buildings inside a metropolis. Here's how you tackle it:

1. Grenade barrages: Launch a synchronised grenade barrage into each building before entering.
2. Clear room by room: Send in infantry squads to clear each room methodically, employing grenades and close-quarters fighting techniques.
3. Secure and flank: Once a building is secured, move on to the next one, employing flanking

movements inside buildings to escape hostile ambushes.

Urban warfare is a violent ballet of clearing structures, seizing objectives, and adjusting to close-quarter battle.

The Art of the Offensive

By grasping the fundamentals of offensive planning, breaking enemy defenses, and fighting successfully in urban areas, you've become a strong offensive commander. Remember, a successful attack involves a mix of strategy, tactical flexibility, and the capacity to adjust to the ever-changing battlefield.

In the following chapter, we'll change gears and cover defensive methods and tactics. We'll learn how to construct fortifications, withstand enemy attacks, and employ defensive tactics to hold the line and emerge triumphant. Remember, soldier, a well-rounded leader thrives in both offensive and defense. Now, let's make you prepared to withstand whatever storm the adversary throws your way!

CHAPTER 7

Defense: A Fortress Unbreachable - Fortifying Your Positions

In this chapter, we'll change you from a conquering warlord into an immovable object, creating impregnable barriers and resisting opposing attacks with unyielding determination. We'll cover the art of fortification, leveraging topography to your advantage, and organising your troops to change the tide of battle in your favor.

Building Strong Defenses: Sandbags, Bunkers, and Anti-Tank Obstacles

A well-fortified position may alter the tide of combat. Here's how to design fortifications that will make your opponents think twice before attacking:

Sandbags: These widely accessible fortifications offer basic cover for your soldiers. Utilize them to build shooting positions and defend your soldiers from enemy small weapons fire.
 Bunkers: Offer higher protection compared to sandbags. Bunkers may be staffed by machine guns, infantry squads, or even anti-tank armament, forming fortified positions that can stave off enemy attacks.
 Anti-Tank Obstacles: Hedges, tank traps, and minefields may greatly restrict enemy armor mobility. Utilize these barriers intelligently to lead opposing tanks into kill zones where your anti-tank armament may wreak havoc.

Fortifications in Action:

Imagine you're charged with defending a critical bridge against enemy troops. Here's how to reinforce your position:

1. Sandbag your flanks: Utilize sandbags to build shooting positions along the bridge's sides, giving cover for your men.
2. Bunker the center: Construct a central bunker on the bridge to house a machine gun squad or anti-tank armament, establishing the anchor of your defense.
3. Mine the approaches: Place minefields before the bridge to hamper opposing armor and create a kill zone for your anti-tank troops.

Remember, a well-layered defense with a variety of fortifications is significantly more effective than depending on a single aspect.

Utilizing Terrain: Height Advantages, Cover, and Choke Points

The battlefield itself might be your best friend. Here's how to exploit the geography to your defensive advantage:

Height Advantage: Occupying higher land gives greater fields of fire and protection for your soldiers. Utilize hills and high spots to control the battlefield.

Cover is Key: Don't leave your soldiers exposed on open terrain. Utilize buildings, trees, and natural formations as cover to reduce losses from hostile fire.

Choke Points: Identify tight routes, bridges, or defiles that the opponent must cross through. Fortify these choke spots to funnel enemy troops into death zones where you may unleash your weaponry.

Terrain in Action:

Imagine you're guarding a small community situated between rolling hills. Here's how to exploit the terrain:

1. Occupy the high ground: Position your infantry teams on top of the hills, enabling them to control the surrounding region with their fire.

2. Fortify the settlement: Utilize the structures inside the hamlet as defensive positions, creating a network of linked fortresses.

3. Bridge choke point: Focus your defenses on the bridge heading into the settlement, turning it into a death zone for your anti-tank armament.

By knowing the terrain and exploiting it to your advantage, you may considerably boost your defenses and make it a nightmare for your enemies to assault.

Repelling Enemy Attacks: Coordinating Infantry, Vehicles, and Artillery Support

A good defense isn't only about walls and terrain. Here's how to successfully organise your soldiers to resist enemy assaults:

Infantry Backbone: The basis of your defense is your infantry. Utilize them to man fortifications, combat enemy soldiers in close quarters, and hold the line.

Vehicle assistance: Tanks and armored vehicles may give important assistance by flanking opposing troops, breaking up infantry assaults, and attacking hostile armor.

Artillery Barrages: Utilize artillery proactively to weaken enemy positions before they reach your defenders. Coordinate artillery fire with other defensive tactics for optimum effect.

Defense in Action:

The adversary conducts a full-frontal attack on your bridge defense. Here's how to resist them:

1. soldiers holds the line: Your soldiers in the sandbags and bunkers unleash fire, suppressing enemy advances and inflicting significant losses.
2. Tank flanking: Send a flanking force using your tanks to attack the enemy's rear, generating surprise and spoiling their assault.
3. Artillery support: Call in a pre-emptive artillery fire on the opposing troops as they

approach the bridge, weakening their resolve before they ever reach your positions.

Beyond the Basics: Advanced Defensive Tactics

While these key concepts build a strong foundation, there's more to defensive mastery:

Reserves and Reinforcements: Hold some forces in reserve to react to unexpected enemy breakthroughs or reinforce vulnerable positions.
Layered Defenses: Don't depend on a single defensive line. Create a tiered defense with fallback locations to slow down the enemy approach and inflict maximum fatalities.
Deception and Misdirection: Utilize smoke grenades and decoy positions to fool the opponent about your genuine force size and placement.

Adapting to the Enemy

A good defense is versatile. Here's how to alter your tactics depending on the opposing force composition:

  Heavy Armor: Focus on deploying anti-tank weapons, minefields, and coordinated artillery attacks to oppose enemy armor offensives.
  Large Infantry Forces: Utilize well-fortified positions with machine guns and enough cover to mow down opposing infantry waves.
  Flanking Maneuvers: Be prepared to transfer your reserves and rearrange troops to counter enemy flanking efforts.

Defense is a Dynamic Art

Defense in Men of War is a continual process, involving constant adaptability and strategic decision-making. By employing powerful fortifications, manipulating the terrain, and directing your men properly, you may make any location into an impregnable fortress. Remember, a great defense may be just as satisfying – and tactically vital – as a well-executed offence.

CHAPTER 8

Mastering the Art of Direct Control - Taking the Wheel

In this chapter, we'll examine the skill of taking the wheel of individual troops, providing you the potential to undertake high-risk, high-reward operations that may swing the balances of combat in your favor.

When to Use Direct Control: Precision Maneuvers and Tactical Advantages

Direct control lets you to control a single unit directly, providing particular movement instructions and shooting orders beyond the conventional squad-level controls. While strong, it comes at the expense of surrendering total control of your force. Here's when direct control shines:

Precision movements: Utilize direct control to conduct movements that squad-level orders could struggle with. This may involve flanking tactics through confined locations, slipping snipers into secret positions, or leading a lone tank across a minefield.

Tactical Advantages: Direct control enables for split-second decision-making. You may respond to scenarios on the fly, including commanding a tank to swiftly reverse out of an ambush or instructing a platoon to toss a bomb into a certain window.

Direct Control in Action:

Imagine you're storming a highly entrenched opposing position. Here's how direct control may help:

1. Tank flanking: Take direct control of a tank and employ its greater mobility to flank the opposing fortifications and strike their rear.
2. Sniper infiltration: Directly direct a sniper team, slipping them into a secret location to destroy enemy leaders or high-value targets.
3. Grenade surprise: Take control of a grenadier and toss a surprise grenade through a window, clearing out entrenched enemy forces.

Remember, direct control is a strong tool for certain circumstances, not a substitute for strategic squad-level management.

Commanding Individual Units: Tank Sniping, Grenadier Raids, and Squad Support

While direct control allows for fine management of every unit, several strategies are especially suited for this approach:

Tank Sniping: Utilize direct control to methodically target your tank's main gun against weak places in opponent armor or vulnerable enemy locations.

Grenadier Raids: Directly control a grenadier to hurl precision grenades into structures or defences, enhancing their impact.

Squad Support: Take temporary control of a squad to offer suppression fire or take out a particular enemy position while your main army advances.

Utilizing Direct Control Effectively:

Here are some more recommendations for maximizing the advantages of direct control:

Hotkeys: Utilize hotkeys to move between squad-level control and direct control for a smooth transition.

Minimap Awareness: Maintain awareness of the battlefield while directly managing a unit. Don't become so concentrated on the micro that you overlook the macro problem.

Use it Sparingly: Direct control is a wonderful weapon, but don't disregard your whole army.

Utilize it for particular scenarios and transition back to squad-level management for general coordination.

The Risks and Rewards of Direct Control: Micromanagement and Efficiency

Direct control gives great tactical benefits, but there are drawbacks to consider:

Micromanagement: Focusing on a single unit might lead to disregarding your whole army. Ensure you don't get mired down in micromanagement and lose sight of the greater picture.
Efficiency: Switching between direct control and squad-level control might disturb your flow and perhaps slow down your decision-making.

Balancing the Risks and Rewards:

The key to mastering direct control comes in striking the proper balance. Utilize it wisely for high-impact movements, but don't forget your overall army management. Practice moving between direct control and squad-level control effectively to optimise its advantages without losing overall combat awareness.

Direct Control: A Powerful Tool in Your Arsenal

By knowing the benefits and limits of direct control, you've added another weapon to your strategic armoury. Utilize it efficiently at those vital times that may swing the tide of war. Remember, a well-timed direct control move may be the difference between success and failure.

Beyond the Basics: Advanced Direct Control Techniques

While we've studied the main uses of direct control, there are many more ways to exploit this strong tool for tactical advantage. Here are some advanced skills to master:

Combined Unit Control: Utilize direct control in combination with squad-level orders. For example, directly control a tank to lead an attack while commanding your infantry team to follow behind it for assistance.

Decoy Maneuvers: Use a directly commanded unit like a light tank or jeep as a decoy to divert opposing fire away from your main force.

Ambush Tactics: Take direct control of a unit like a sniper or anti-tank squad and deploy them in a covert spot to launch a deadly surprise strike on unsuspecting foes.

Mastering these advanced methods will enable you to conduct complicated movements and outwit your opponents.

Specialization and Unit Roles

Different unit types benefit from direct control in diverse ways:

Tanks: Utilize direct control for precision shooting, moving through confined places, and conducting fast retreats from perilous circumstances.
Infantry Squads: Directly direct infantry squads for storming certain structures, flanking via small tunnels, or hurling explosives into selected spots.
Support Units: Take control of support units like mortars or artillery to modify their fire angles and target particular enemy locations with precision accuracy.

Understanding how each unit type benefits from direct control helps you to optimise its efficacy in certain scenarios.

When Not to Use Direct Control

While appealing, there are situations when direct control might impair your overall strategy:

Large-Scale fights: Don't get bogged down in micromanaging individual troops during large-scale fights. Focus on squad-level management and strategic decision-making to preserve overall battlefield awareness.
Base Management: Direct control isn't good for controlling base development or unit manufacturing. Utilize the specific menus for these activities to preserve efficiency.
Reinforcements: Don't become obsessed on directly commanding reinforcements as they arrive. Quickly incorporate them into your current structures for a seamless transition.

understanding when to avoid direct control is just as crucial as understanding when to wield it.

Mastering Direct Control: Practice Makes Perfect

Direct control requires practice to perfect. Here are some suggestions to develop your skills:

Start Small: Begin by exercising direct control with a single unit in skirmishes against AI opponents. Gradually increase the complexity as you develop familiarity.

Hotkey Mastery: Mastering hotkeys for switching between troops and control modes is vital for smooth transitions and efficient gaming.

Practice Makes Perfect: The more you apply direct control, the more comfortable and efficient you'll become. Experiment with different strategies and unit kinds in various circumstances.

By spending time to practice and mastering these advanced tactics, you'll convert direct control from a situational tool into a weapon of strategic genius.

The Art of Direct Control

Direct control adds a whole new level to your tactical arsenal in Men of War. By recognising its strengths and limitations, applying advanced strategies, and tailoring your approach with various unit types, you may exploit this potent instrument to attain battlefield domination. Remember, a well-timed direct control move may be the difference between a strategic stalemate and a decisive triumph.

PART 3

BEYOND THE BASICS

CHAPTER 10

The Road to Mastery - Advanced Techniques and Strategies

Congratulations are in order! You've mastered the fundamentals of Men of War and are ready to develop your talents. This chapter goes into sophisticated strategies that will improve your gaming from qualified commander to battlefield master.

Combined Arms Tactics: Coordinating Infantry, Vehicles, and Support for Maximum Effect

Men of War isn't simply about controlling a single troop type. True expertise resides in wielding a combined weapons force, when infantry, vehicles, and support units operate together harmoniously. Here's how to make your army a coherent combat machine:

Infantry as the Backbone: They may not be the flashiest troops, but well-positioned infantry are the cornerstone of your force. Use them to take objectives, maintain vital locations, and combat opposing forces. Exploit their strengths: Rifle squads for suppressing fire, engineers for repairs and demolitions, and anti-tank squads to fight opposing armor.

Armored Fists: Tanks are formidable attacking instruments, yet vulnerable alone. Use them in concert with infantry support. soldiers may sweep opposing soldiers out of structures and woodlands, giving safe access for your tanks. Smoke grenades may further hamper opponent eyesight as your tanks approach. Remember, different tanks fulfil various tasks. Heavier tanks thrive in head-on assaults, whereas lighter ones offer flanking maneuvers or mobile fire support.

Support Symphony: Don't underestimate the strength of support units. Artillery barrages may soften enemy positions before an infantry attack. Mortars deliver constant harassing over wide terrain. Anti-air units guarantee your skies are clean for bombers and recon aircraft. Learn the strengths and limitations of each support unit and integrate them strategically.

Mastering the Art of Combined Arms:

Combined Assault: This is the bread and butter of combined weapons. Suppress enemy positions with artillery or mortars. Move infantry under smoke cover to clear buildings and close the distance. Follow up with tanks to exploit the weakened enemy line. This coordinated strategy optimises your firepower while reducing losses.

Armored Spearhead: Use tanks as a spearhead to burst past opposing lines. Precede them with engineer teams to remove minefields and impediments. Have flanking infantry squads ready to mop up remaining enemy pockets.

Remember, even the mightiest tank can be crippled by infantry bazookas or mines.

Ambush Maestro: Lure enemy tanks into traps using strategically placed infantry squads with anti-tank weapons. Suppress enemy infantry with flanking fire while your anti-tank squads unleash their firepower on the exposed enemy armor. Remember, well-placed mines can also be devastating to unsuspecting tanks.

Resource Management and Base Building (if applicable)

Some Men of War campaigns and multiplayer maps feature base building elements. Here's a crash course on resource management and base building:

Know Your Resources: Most games revolve around capturing strategic points that generate resources like manpower and munitions. Secure these points early and prioritize their defense.

Building a Strong Foundation: Start with basic structures like barracks to produce infantry and factories for vehicles. Research upgrades to improve unit capabilities as resources allow.

Defense is Key: Don't neglect defenses! Build fortifications like trenches, bunkers, and anti-tank guns to protect your base from enemy attacks.

Multiplayer Strategies: Adapting to Online Challenges and Player Tactics

The online battlefield presents unique challenges. Here are some tips to thrive against human opponents:

Scouting is Crucial: Unlike AI, human players are unpredictable. Constantly scout enemy movements using infantry squads and recon units. This intel helps you anticipate enemy tactics and formulate your own strategies.

Adapt and Counter: Be prepared to shift your tactics based on your opponent's playstyle. Are they turtling with heavy defenses? Focus on siege tactics. Do they favor fast armored assaults? Build anti-tank defenses and mobile infantry squads.

Exploit Player Mistakes: Everyone makes mistakes. Watch for enemy overextensions or poorly positioned units. Be ruthless and capitalize on these opportunities to gain a significant advantage.

Communication is Key: If playing in teams, utilize the in-game chat and voice communication to coordinate attacks, share intel, and call for support. Teamwork is essential for victory.

Practice Makes Perfect

Mastering these advanced skills needs effort and practice. Experiment with varied strategies in single-player fights to develop your abilities. Don't get disheartened by defeats in multiplayer; examine your blunders and change your methods. Watch replays of your own games and those of skilled players to find areas for growth.

The path to mastery is lengthy, but with commitment and these advanced methods as your guide, you'll be dominating the battlefield in no time. Remember, a good commander is continuously learning and adjusting. Good luck, soldier!

Advanced Unit Control Techniques

Having covered combined weapons tactics and strategic resource management, let's go further into sophisticated unit control strategies. Mastering them will raise your micro-management abilities and enable you to respond fast in the heat of combat.

Unit Formations: Formations are vital for enhancing unit performance in varied conditions.

Experiment with different arrangements including line formations for open field confrontations, wedge formations for breaching enemy lines, and skirmish formations for loose flanking movements. Mastering formations helps you to maximise unit firepower and reduce fatalities.

Sophisticated Unit Commands: Utilize the sophisticated command interface to explore the full power of your troops. Use suppressive fire instructions to trap down enemy, create rally points to move fleeing forces to advantageous places, and deploy bayonet charges for close-quarter shock tactics. Remember, learning these orders takes practice and becomes second nature in the pandemonium of war.

Micromanaging Specialists: Certain units profit from intensive micromanagement. Exploit the unique talents of engineers to swiftly fix damaged vehicles or take crucial sites. Use smoke grenades skillfully to hinder opponent eyesight and hide your unit movements.

Remember, micromanagement should be employed strategically, not replace well-coordinated unit formations.

Terrain Exploitation: The battlefield environment plays a key role. Use trees and buildings for shelter, and high terrain for defensive benefits. Indirect fire units like mortars are most effective when positioned on slopes with unobstructed lines of sight. Remember, smart terrain exploitation may swing the tide of combat.

Mastering Maneuvers and Combat Strategies

Flanking Maneuvers: Don't simply assault head-on. Use flanking tactics to outmaneuver your attacker. This entails sending troops around opponent flanks to attack their weaker rear sides. Flanking movements may be deadly, particularly against armor-heavy forces.

Artillery Deception: Use artillery barrages strategically. Employ a rapid bombardment on a single place to draw enemy forces into the open, then follow up with a surprise assault from another direction. Artillery may also be employed to suppress enemy fortifications before an infantry attack.

Smoke Screens and Ambush Tactics: Smoke grenades are useful instruments. Use them to hide your unit movements during an attack or to cover a retreat. Smoke may also be utilised to create killing zones where you rain down artillery or mortar fire on unsuspecting foes.

Combined Arms Retreat: A well-executed retreat may be a worthwhile manoeuvre. When confronting overwhelming odds, fall back behind smoke cover while deploying artillery or mortar fire to hamper the enemy pursuit. This permits you to recover and counter-attack when the moment arrives.

Remember, Knowledge is Power

Men of War rewards players who possess a comprehensive grasp of the game's rules and unit capabilities. Here are some extra suggestions to enhance your strategic knowledge:

Study Unit Statistics: Familiarize yourself with the strengths and weaknesses of each unit. This information lets you make educated judgements regarding unit duties and target selection.

Learn Unit Veterancy: Units acquire veterancy via battle experience, making them more effective. A seasoned team will outperform a fresh one. Protect your experienced troops at all costs, since they constitute the backbone of your battle force.

Explore Advanced Tactics: The internet is a rich resource of advanced tactics and methods. Watch replays of elite gamers, study online instructions, and join in online forums to learn from experienced players.

CONCLUSION

You've navigated the boot camp, polished your tactical skills, and emerged triumphant from numerous engagements. Now, as you stand set to rule the multiplayer battlefield or overcome the greatest single-player tasks, here are some parting words to drive you towards mastery:

Embrace the Learning Curve: Men of War is a game with great complexity. Don't be disheartened by first setbacks. Embrace the learning curve, examine your blunders, and enhance your approach. Every struggle offers a vital lesson, and every failure lays the road for future wins.

Practice Makes Perfect: Sharpen your talents via persistent practice. Experiment with varied approaches in single-player battles and multiplayer contests. The more you play, the more comfortable you'll get with unit control, resource management, and strategic decision-making under duress.

Seek Knowledge and Inspiration: The internet is a large storehouse of Men of War knowledge. Watch replays of experienced players, dig into online forums and groups, and examine complex strategies manuals. Learn from the experiences of others and implement excellent methods into your own toolbox.

develop Your Own route: While established tactics are useful, don't be afraid to explore and develop your own route. Adapt strategies to your playstyle and exploit unique possibilities on the battlefield. Innovation and inventiveness may lead to unforeseen successes.

Sportsmanship and Community: The online community depends on sportsmanship and mutual respect. Be a nice victor and a polite loser. Offer helpful comments to other players and learn from their techniques. A cheerful mindset encourages a healthy and happy internet experience.

The Neverending Journey: Men of War is a continually changing game. New maps, modifications, and tactics appear all the time. Embrace the continuing learning process, keep yourself current with the newest advances, and continue to push yourself with new experiences.

Beyond the Battlefield: The abilities you learn in Men of War may transcend to other real-time strategy games. Your mastery of unit control, resource management, and strategic thinking will serve you well in a number of gaming scenarios.

The exhilaration of triumph: Few things compare to the exhilaration of outsmarting your opponent and gaining a hard-fought triumph. Celebrate your victories, but remember that every win provides a chance to perfect your talents and aim for even bigger achievements.

In Conclusion: Men of War is a wonderful experience that provides unlimited strategic depth and tactical options. By embracing the learning curve, developing your talents, and nurturing a passion for information, you'll be well on your way to being a master of the battlefield.

APPENDIX

This appendix serves as a thorough reference for novice players stepping into the realm of Men of War.

Appendix A: Unit Reference Guide (By Faction)

Note: This section is useful only if your game has different playable factions with various unit kinds. If your game contains a single unified force, this part may be skipped.

This guide gives a fast reference for the numerous troops available in Men of War, grouped by faction. For each unit, offer a short summary of its job, strengths, and limitations.

Faction: Soviet Union

Rifle Squad: The backbone of the Soviet army. These adaptable troops excel at holding terrain and suppressing opposing positions. They are weak against tanks and need backup from other troops.

T-34 Medium Tank: A workhorse of the Soviet armored army. The T-34 offers a strong blend of firepower and armor, making it useful against most infantry and light vehicles. However, it is susceptible against bigger German tanks.

Katyusha Rocket Launcher: A potent indirect fire device that fires destructive barrages of rockets. Effective in softening enemy defenses and suppressing wide regions. Vulnerable to counter-battery fire and needs protection against flanking movements.

Repeat the procedure for all playable factions in your game.

Appendix B: Glossary of Terms

This glossary describes widely used terminology used in Men of War.

Armor: Refers to the protective plate of vehicles and certain infantry units. Higher armor levels give higher resistance against hostile fire.

Artillery: Long-range indirect fire units that pound enemy locations with shells or rockets.

Base Building: The process of constructing buildings to create troops, research upgrades, and defend your region (relevant only if the game incorporates base building mechanics).

Combined Arms: A military doctrine that stresses the coordinated deployment of infantry, vehicles, and support forces to optimise combat effectiveness.

Flanking Maneuver: An attack that bypasses the enemy's main force and targets their weaker flanks or rear.

Infantry: The foot troops of an army, tasked for seizing objectives, battling opposing infantry, and giving assistance to other units.

Line of Sight: The unimpeded road between a unit and its target, vital for engaging in battle.

Micromanagement: The act of giving precise directives to individual troops or small groups.

Multiplayer: The form of play when you compete against other human gamers online.

Rally Point: A specified site where fleeing forces regroup and prepare to rejoin the fight.

Resources: Materials necessary to generate units and erect buildings (e.g., people, ammunition, gasoline).

Scouting: The act of acquiring information about enemy locations and movements utilising recon troops or infantry patrols.

Single-Player: The form of play when you battle against AI-controlled adversaries.

Suppression: The employment of continuous fire to pin down opposing forces, decreasing their effectiveness and morale.

Tank: Armored battle vehicles, the principal offensive force in most militaries. They are formidable against infantry and light vehicles but might be susceptible to anti-tank weaponry and flanking tactics.

Veterancy: A mechanism that awards troops with combat experience, making them more effective in battle. Veteran troops have greater accuracy, morale, and battle resistance.

Expand this list to cover all the crucial phrases a new player could meet while playing Men of War.

Appendix C: Recommended Resources: Online Guides, Community Hubs, and Tutorials

The internet provides a multitude of materials to improve your Men of War experience. This section contains a handpicked collection of excellent web resources:

Official Game Forums: The official forums offered by the game creator are a wonderful location to get official news, problem complaints, and conversations with other players and developers.

Online Strategy Guides: Numerous websites give thorough strategy guides for Men of War. These guides include strategy, unit breakdowns, and advanced gaming ideas.

Community Hubs and Wikis: Dedicated community hubs and wikis give complete information about the game, including unit statistics, map data, and user-created guides.

Video Tutorials: YouTube and other video-sharing platforms provide countless tutorials prepared by expert gamers. These tutorials give graphic representations of techniques and methods.

www.ingramcontent.com/pod-product-compliance
Lightning Source LLC
Chambersburg PA
CBHW071212240526
45470CB00018B/1777